HORSES

The THOROUGHBRED Horse

by John Diedrich

Consultant:
Gay Fisher
Director of Marketing and Communications
Thoroughbred Owners and
Breeders Association
Lexington, Kentucky

Capstone press

Mankato, Minnesota

Edge Books are published by Capstone Press,
151 Good Counsel Drive, P.O. Box 669, Mankato, Minnesota 56002.
www.capstonepress.com

Library of Congress Cataloging-in-Publication Data
Diedrich, John.
    The thoroughbred horse / by John Diedrich.
    p. cm.—(Edge books. Horses)
    Includes bibliographical references and index.
    ISBN 0-7368-3768-X (hardcover)
    1. Thoroughbred horse—Juvenile literature. I. Title. II. Series.
SF293.T5D54 2005
636.1'32—dc22   2004019418

Summary: Describes Thoroughbred horses, including their history, physical features, and primary uses.

Editorial Credits
Angie Kaelberer, editor; Juliette Peters, designer; Deirdre Barton,
    photo researcher; Scott Thoms, photo editor

Photo Credits
All Posters/J. Wootton, 6
Capstone Press/Gary Sundermeyer, 24
Corbis, 26; Bettmann, 9; Jerry Cooke, 25; Reuters/John Sommers, 23
© 2004 Mark J. Barrett, cover, back cover, 5, 10, 13, 16–17, 29
PhotoDisc, 11
Sharon P. Fibelkorn, 14, 19, 20

1 2 3 4 5 6 10 09 08 07 06 05

Table of Contents

FEATURES

Chapter 1

Born to Race

When people think of Thoroughbreds, they think of horse racing. Most racehorses are Thoroughbreds. Thoroughbreds gallop around racetracks at speeds up to 40 miles (64 kilometers) per hour.

The Thoroughbred is a young horse breed. The breed has existed for only 300 years. Some horse breeds began thousands of years ago.

In the 1500s, horse racing was a popular sport in England. The fastest horses at that time were Arabians. English kings and other noblemen wanted to create an even faster horse breed.

Learn about:
- ★ **Famous ancestors**
- ★ **Early champions**
- ★ **American Jockey Club**

Thoroughbreds are famous for their speed.

The Darley Arabian was an important ancestor of today's Thoroughbreds.

Three Important Stallions

In 1688, Captain Robert Byerley captured a black Arabian stallion during a war in Hungary. After the war, he took the stallion home to England. The horse was called the Byerley Turk.

In 1704, Thomas Darley bought an Arabian stallion in Syria. He sent it to England. This horse became known as the Darley Arabian.

In 1724, an Arabian stallion was born in North Africa. The king of Tunis gave the young horse to King Louis XV of France. Englishman Edward Coke later bought the stallion. In 1729, Coke sold the horse to the Earl of Godolphin. People called the stallion the Godolphin Arabian.

These three Arabian stallions began the Thoroughbred breed. Their owners bred them to English racing mares. The stallions were sources of speed and spirit. The mares provided size and strength.

Coming to America

In 1730, Bulle Rock became the first Thoroughbred stallion brought to the British colonies in North America. His father was the Darley Arabian, and his grandfather was the Byerley Turk.

In 1805, the stallion Sir Archy was born in Virginia. He became the top racehorse in the United States. Later, Sir Archy's owners used him to establish the Thoroughbred breed in the United States. He also was an important ancestor of the American Quarter Horse breed.

Moving West

Most early U.S. Thoroughbred breeders lived in Virginia. In the 1800s, settlers began to move west. They took their Thoroughbreds with them. Tennessee and Kentucky became top horse-producing states. Thoroughbreds still graze on the bluegrass pastures of Kentucky.

By the 1820s, Kentucky had many racetracks. The town of Lexington became famous for horse breeding and racing.

Man o'War

Many racing experts believe Man o'War was the greatest racehorse ever. This chestnut horse was born in 1917. He had a stride that was 28 feet (8.5 meters) long.

In two years of racing, Man o'War won 20 of his 21 races. After he retired, Man o'War sired many top racers. His son War Admiral won the Triple Crown in 1937.

When Man o'War died in 1947, his owners placed his body in a large coffin. Racing fans from around the world came to say good-bye to the great horse. People still visit his grave at the Kentucky Horse Park in Lexington.

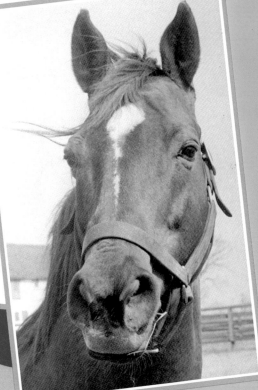

Even as foals, Thoroughbreds are athletic and spirited.

Jockey Club

In 1894, a group of Thoroughbred owners formed the American Jockey Club in New York City. Owners register their Thoroughbreds' names and ancestry with this organization.

Today, the American Jockey Club accepts about 37,000 new foal registrations each year. This number makes the Thoroughbred the third largest breed in the United States.

Chapter 2

Speed and Style

The Thoroughbred is a tall breed. Horses are measured in hands. One hand equals 4 inches (10 centimeters). An average Thoroughbred's height is 16 hands at the withers, which is the top of the shoulders.

Built for Speed

The Thoroughbred's body is well suited for racing. The Thoroughbred's long, sloped shoulders and powerful hindquarters give it a longer stride than horses of other breeds. Thoroughbreds also have long, powerful muscles that allow them to explode with speed.

Learn about:
* ★ Size
* ★ Strong racers
* ★ Colors

The Thoroughbred has a longer stride than many other breeds do.

Some tall horses are heavy, but the Thoroughbred is sleek and slender. The Thoroughbred's slender body helps it run fast.

▼ Common Thoroughbred colors are (left to right) bay, brown, and chestnut.

A Handsome Breed

The Thoroughbred's appearance is a reminder that its ancestors were Arabians. Arabian horses are known for their beauty. Thoroughbreds have wide foreheads and large, dark eyes. Thoroughbreds also have thinner, longer necks than most breeds.

Thoroughbreds can be many colors. The most common colors are brown, bay, and chestnut. Bay horses are red-brown with black lower legs and black manes and tails. Chestnut is a shade of copper or red.

Thoroughbreds can also be black, gray, white, palomino, or roan. Palomino horses are tan with lighter manes and tails. Roan horses have coats of a solid color mixed with white hairs.

Personality

Thoroughbreds' personalities also make them good racehorses. Thoroughbreds are intelligent and spirited. They seem to enjoy the competition of racing. Off the track, most Thoroughbreds are gentle and cooperative. They tend to form a strong bond with their trainers or handlers.

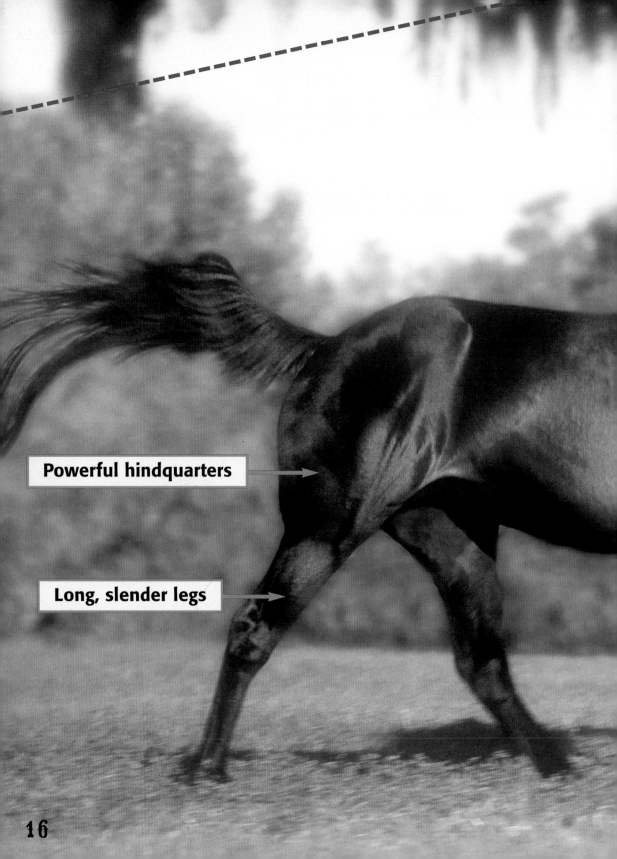

Powerful hindquarters

Long, slender legs

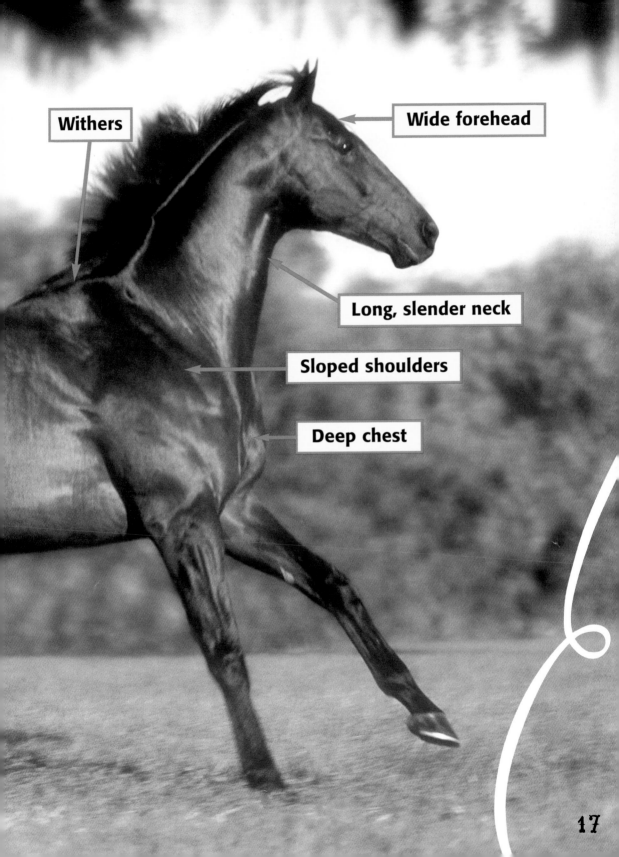

Withers

Wide forehead

Long, slender neck

Sloped shoulders

Deep chest

17

Chapter 3

Training for the Track

Thoroughbred racehorses begin their training shortly after birth. The horses are broke for riding late in their first year. By age 2, many Thoroughbreds are ready to race.

Race Training

Experienced riders called trainers work with Thoroughbred racehorses. The trainers decide how the horses will be worked each day.

The trainer works with an exercise rider. The trainer tells the exercise rider how far and how fast to ride the Thoroughbred.

Learn about:
★ Trainers
★ Learning to race
★ Racing careers

An exercise rider works with a racehorse each day.

An exercise rider ponies a young horse around the track.

Some days, the horse is ponied around the track. While riding another horse, the exercise rider leads the Thoroughbred around the track. The exercise rider also takes the horse for long jogs and slow gallops around the track. These exercises get the Thoroughbred in racing shape.

Young Thoroughbreds in good condition can gallop at a high speed, or breeze. When the Thoroughbred is breezing, the trainer times it with a stopwatch. The trainer times the horse to make sure it is getting faster. If not, the trainer changes the horse's training.

Racing

Thoroughbreds may enter their first races as 2-year-olds. These races are called baby races. Thoroughbreds usually run in only a few baby races. Young horses that are raced too much can become injured.

At age 3, Thoroughbreds can enter more races. Some owners retire their horses after the second year of racing. Others race their horses as long as they continue to win. Some Thoroughbreds still race at age 10 or older.

Chapter 4

Thoroughbreds in Action

Thoroughbreds race on dirt or grass tracks. Races are measured in furlongs. Each furlong is one-eighth of a mile (.2 kilometer). Races are usually 4 to 9 furlongs in length.

The most famous Thoroughbred race is held each year at Churchill Downs in Louisville, Kentucky. The first Saturday in May, the world's fastest 3-year-old Thoroughbreds race in the Kentucky Derby.

The Kentucky Derby is the first of three races called the Triple Crown. The second race is the Preakness Stakes in Baltimore, Maryland. The last race is the Belmont Stakes. The Belmont is run at Belmont Park in New York.

Learn about:
★ Tracks
★ Triple Crown
★ Jumping and dressage

In 2004, Smarty Jones (front) won the Kentucky Derby.

Triple Crown winners are rare. Since 1875, only 11 horses have won the Triple Crown. The last horses to win the Triple Crown were Secretariat in 1973, Seattle Slew in 1977, and Affirmed in 1978. Since then, several horses have won the Derby and the Preakness but have lost the Belmont.

The Triple Crown races are the most famous horse races. But there are many other races. Some Thoroughbreds travel around the world during their racing careers.

Eye on the Prize

Racehorses compete for prize money called a purse. Each race has a purse that is split among owners of the top five horses. Some races have purses of $1 million or more.

In North America, the largest purse is at the Breeders' Cup World Thoroughbred Championships. The top racehorses compete at this event in late October. Its eight races offer purses of about $14 million.

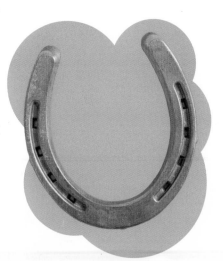

Secretariat

In 1973, a large chestnut Thoroughbred won the Triple Crown. His name was Secretariat.

Secretariat was born in 1970 in Virginia. By age 2, he stood 16.2 hands and weighed 1,200 pounds (544 kilograms).

The big red horse had an amazing racing career. Secretariat set track records with his winning times at the Kentucky Derby and the Preakness. At the Belmont, he finished the race 31 lengths ahead of the second-place finisher. His time of 2 minutes, 24 seconds set a world record.

Secretariat sired championship foals before he died in 1989. In 2004, his great-great-grandson Smarty Jones won both the Kentucky Derby and the Preakness Stakes.

Some riders use Thoroughbreds in fox hunting events.

Other Competitions

Not all Thoroughbreds are racehorses. Thoroughbreds also do well at jumping, fox hunting, and dressage. In dressage competitions, horses perform a series of advanced movements.

Thoroughbreds also compete in horse shows. Thoroughbreds do well in both English and Western riding events.

Thoroughbred Care

Like all horses, Thoroughbreds need a great deal of care. Top racehorses live in air-conditioned stables with trainers and veterinarians on call. Horses used for jumping, dressage, or shows may not live in such grand surroundings. But they still need a barn or stable for shelter and a large pasture where they can graze and run.

The thrill of the Triple Crown excites racing fans each spring. At the center of it all are the Thoroughbreds. These strong, graceful athletes are born to run.

The Thoroughbred Horse

History: The Thoroughbred breed began about 300 years ago when people brought Arabian stallions to England and bred them to the local mares. The first Thoroughbred came to North America in 1730.

Height: 15 to 17 hands (about 5 feet or 1.5 meters) tall at the withers. Each hand equals 4 inches (10 centimeters).

Weight: 900 to 1,200 pounds (408 to 544 kilograms)

Colors: bay, brown, chestnut, black, gray, white, palomino, roan

Features: tall, lean body; slender, well-muscled neck; long, slender legs; deep chest; wide forehead; large eyes

Personality: intelligent, spirited

Abilities: Thoroughbreds are best known for racing. They are also used for shows, jumping, fox hunting, and dressage.

Life span: 20 to 30 years

Glossary

ancestor (AN-sess-tur)—a member of a breed that lived a long time ago

dressage (druh-SAHJ)—a riding style in which horses complete a pattern while doing advanced moves

foal (FOHL)—a horse that is less than 1 year old

gallop (GAL-uhp)—a fast run

hindquarter (HIND-kwor-tur)—the part of a horse where the back leg and rump connect to the body

mare (MAIR)—an adult female horse

register (REJ-uh-stur)—to enter a horse's name and ancestry with an official club

roan (ROHN)—a solid color hair coat mixed with white hairs

stallion (STAL-yuhn)—an adult male horse that can be used for breeding

Read More

Baker, Kent. *Thoroughbred Racing*. Horse Library. Philadelphia: Chelsea House, 2002.

Dubowski, Mark, and Cathy East Dubowski. *A Horse Named Seabiscuit*. All Aboard Reading. New York: Grosset and Dunlap, 2003.

Kelley, Brent P. *Horse Breeds of the World*. Horse Library. Philadelphia: Chelsea House, 2002.

Internet Sites

FactHound offers a safe, fun way to find Internet sites related to this book. All of the sites on FactHound have been researched by our staff.

Here's how:

1. Visit *www.facthound.com*
2. Type in this special code **073683768X** for age-appropriate sites. Or enter a search word related to this book for a more general search.
3. Click on the **Fetch It** button.

FactHound will fetch the best sites for you!

Index